LET'S GO TEAM:
Cheer, Dance, March

LET'S GO TEAM:
Cheer, Dance, March

Techniques of
CHEERLEADING

Craig Peters

Mason Crest Publishers
Philadelphia

To Alexandra: Always remember to keep your head up and smile.

Mason Crest Publishers, Inc.
370 Reed Road
Broomall, PA 19008
(866) MCP-BOOK (toll free)
www.masoncrest.com

2 3 4 5 6 7 8 9 10

Library of Congress Cataloging-in-Publication Data

Peters, Craig, 1958-
  Techniques of cheerleading / Craig Peters.
      v. cm. — (Let's go team—cheer, dance, march)
Includes index.
Contents: Don't let this happen to you — Hand, arm, and leg positions
— Vocal techniques — Jumps.
  ISBN 1-59084-530-7
  1. Cheerleading—Juvenile literature. [1. Cheerleading.] I. Title.
II. Series.
  LB3635 .P438 2003
  791.6'4—dc21

                                                        2002015951

Produced by
Choptank Syndicate and Chestnut Productions
226 South Washington Street
Easton, Maryland 21601

Project Editors Norman Macht and Mary Hull
Design Lisa Hochstein
Picture Research Mary Hull

Printed and bound in the Hashemite Kingdom of Jordan

OPPOSITE TITLE PAGE

With spotters assisting, bases hold flyers in prep mounts during a competition.

Table of Contents

Don't Let This Happen to You

he time has come, and the pressure is on. Months ago, you decided you were going to try out for the cheerleading squad. You'd been watching the current squad, and you kept telling yourself, "I could do that." You can, too. You have all the athletic skills. You have the determination. You have the personality.

You practiced at home, stretching and training every chance you got. You went to the preliminary meeting when you saw the announcement posted on the school wall. You met with the coach, talked to some of your friends on the squad, and prepared yourself mentally for a lot of work.

More and more young people are being drawn to cheerleading each year. In 2002, nearly half a million cheerleaders attended summer cheer camps to learn new skills and practice their technique.

A SAMPLE GRADING FORM

This sample grading form shows how a coach or judge might rate your performance.

ELEMENT   GRADE (1=poor, 2=fair, 3=good, 4=excellent)

PERSONALITY   GRADE _____
How well does the cheerleader maintain eye contact? Does the cheerleader look and sound sincere? Is the cheerleader making a connection with the audience?

SPIRIT   GRADE _____
Does the cheerleader demonstrate enthusiasm? Is the cheerleader able to motivate the crowd?

CHEER MOTIONS   GRADE _____
Are the cheerleader's hand, arm, and leg motions crisp and strong? Do the motions have good placement?

TIMING AND RHYTHM   GRADE _____
Are the cheerleader's movements balanced and flowing? Does the cheerleader's movement appear smooth and natural as opposed to forced and awkward?

APPEARANCE   GRADE _____
Does the cheerleader appear neat and well groomed? Is the cheerleader's outfit neat?

VOCAL PROJECTION   GRADE _____
Is the cheerleader's voice projecting loud and clear without sounding strained or unnatural?

JUMPS   GRADE _____
Is the cheerleader achieving good jump height? Do the jumps show good form? Is the cheerleader able to perform a variety of jumps?

STUNTS   GRADE _____
Are the cheerleader's stunts performed properly? Are the cheerleader's movements crisp and natural instead of forced and labored?

OVERALL PERFORMANCE   GRADE _____
How is the cheerleader's general athletic ability? How is the cheerleader's overall technique?

The week of tryouts came, and you felt like you were in the zone. You did everything possible to maintain a positive attitude. You kept practicing at home, and you could tell that you were in better shape than you were a few months ago.

When tryout day came, you felt great. You had a cheer that you wrote yourself, and you did your own choreography. You had some butterflies in your stomach, but nothing too bad. When it was all over, you talked to some of the other kids at the tryout. They were nervous, too. In fact, it sounded like most of them were far more nervous than you.

With 12 people trying out for six spots on the squad, you felt your chances were far better than 50-50.

When the day came to check the paper on the school bulletin board that announced who made the team, you didn't want to look. You were scared and excited, all at the same time. You almost had to look through your fingers to find out that you didn't make it. Ouch.

How could this happen? What went wrong? Your friends on the team encouraged you to go talk to the coach. She's really nice, they told you. She's the kind of coach you can talk to easily. So you gathered up your courage and went to the coach's office after school.

She was nice, a lot nicer than you expected. She didn't show you your scorecard, but she talked about what was written there.

The coach said you were loud, but you were screeching. The coach said it sounded like you were yelling from the throat, not from your chest. Points off for that one.

Judges don't just look at cheers, jumps, and stunts, they consider enthusiasm and personality, too.

You smiled a lot, but not all the time. A few times during your tryout, the coach said, your face seemed to be concentrating too much on what to do next. You seemed to be worried about the movements you were doing, and working too hard at them.

There were a few other things the coach mentioned to you. Your high V was a little too high, more like a touchdown. Your tuck jump was very good, and you got excellent height, but both feet weren't pointing at the floor.

The coach was encouraging. You were told that it was very close, that had a few of the things you just discussed been better, you probably would have made the squad. If only you'd paid closer attention to all the details.

Paying close attention to the details is what this book is about. You'll find dozens of tips for making good cheerleading better.

The tips in this book aren't just for tryouts, although they'll certainly help you do better at tryouts. They're not just for competitions. They're for anytime you put on the uniform and step out onto the playing field or competition floor. They are techniques you should remember all the time, a powerful toolkit to help you become the very best cheerleader you can be.

Hand, Arm, and Leg Positions

Ask any coach of any team what the most important skills are for that team to know, and most likely you'll get this answer: "the basics."

Even when professional teams have trouble winning, the answer is often for the manager and the coaches to get back to basics. Study the fundamentals. Identify and fix the problems with the fundamentals, and the bigger problems start to take care of themselves.

In this chapter, we look at some of the most basic fundamentals of cheerleading: hand, arm, and leg movements and positions.

Cheerleaders from Bowling Green, Kentucky, demonstrate the hands on hips position. For this position to look symmetrical, each fist must be placed exactly opposite the other.

HAND POSITIONS

There are certain hand positions that are appropriate at certain times while cheerleading. Form a blade while performing a toe touch jump, for example, but use the dagger when you're doing a spread eagle jump. Here are the basic hand positions to remember.

Blade. To form a blade, open your hand flat and press all of your fingers together. It's very much like the kind of position you would hold your hand in while diving into a pool. Make sure your thumb is tucked in tight against

MUSCLE MEMORY

The best way to practice your hand, arm, and leg motions is by watching yourself in a mirror.

Try holding each position in front of the mirror for 20 to 30 seconds as you squeeze your muscles tight. Next, let your body go limp for a second or two. Then close your eyes and try to resume the position correctly again, without looking. When you think it feels right, open your eyes and take a look.

Do you need to make adjustments? If so, make those adjustments and do it again. Did you hit the position just right? Great. Now do it again. As with all training exercises, repetition is key. Stick to it, and you'll get there before you know it.

The goal of an exercise like this is to train your muscles to "know" what each position feels like. Then, when you go to do the position the next time, your muscles will automatically start to take your body where it needs to go so that the position is exactly the way you want it to be.

your hand, too, but keep your thumb on the side of your hand, not tucked over onto your palm.

Let's Go Team Technique Tip: Don't hyperextend your fingers, or else your hand will lose its flatness and start to look like it is curved.

Bucket. To form a bucket, face your palm to the ground, then make a fist. Think of carrying a bucket of water, and you'll get the idea.

Let's Go Team Technique Tip: Imagine that you're holding a stick in your hand while forming a bucket. Be sure to keep that stick parallel with the ground.

Candlestick. A candlestick is very much like a bucket, but your fists should be turned so that the imaginary candle you might be holding is pointing up in the air.

Let's Go Team Technique Tip: Place your thumb by your index and middle fingers, not covering the "swirl" created by your index finger.

Dagger. A dagger is another fist position, except in this case you'll be turning your hand so that it seems as if you're stabbing the air with a dagger. You should also keep your wrist straight, not bent, so that the back of your hand forms a straight line with your forearm, all the way up to your elbow. Your pinkie finger should face ahead.

Let's Go Team Technique Tip: Keep your thumb off to the side, layered over your index and middle fingers. Don't grab your thumb with your other fingers.

ARM MOTIONS

Where do you place your arms? Up here? Down there? Depending on the situation, arm positions can mean all the difference between a good-looking cheer and a sloppy-looking cheer. Here are the basic arm motions you need to learn.

Diagonal. In a diagonal, you're creating a straight line with both arms, except instead of those arms being parallel to the ground, one arm is raised and one arm is lowered. Diagonals can be called left diagonals and right diagonals, depending on which arm is pointing up. One variation of the diagonal is called the broken diagonal, in which you bend one or both of your arms at the elbows to create a shorter line.

Let's Go Team Technique Tip: Practice doing left and right diagonals in front of a mirror. Try to remember how your arms feel when they look to be in the right positions. Close your eyes and try to recreate the exact position for each from just the feel. Before long, you'll be able to match the feel of the position with exactly the way you want it to look.

Hands on hips. This move is exactly what it sounds like. The key here, though, it to make sure that your hands are clasped into fists, and that your fists are exactly opposite each other on your hips. If one fist is higher up on your body than the other, your body will look out of proportion and lopsided.

Let's Go Team Technique Tip: When you practice this in the mirror, draw an imaginary line from one elbow to the other. That line should be parallel with the ground.

Punch up. The punch up is when you take one arm and, while making a fist with your hand, "punch" the air so that your arm is extended straight up. Your other arm

For the punch up, one arm is pointed straight up, while the other is held in the hand on hip position.

should be set in a hand on hip position. There are right punch ups and left punch ups, depending on which arm is pointing into the air. A variation of the punch up is called the punch out, in which your arms are pointed straight ahead rather than straight up.

Let's Go Team Technique Tip: Take a five-foot-long piece of string and tie one end around a pencil and the other end around a small weight. Practice punch ups in front of the mirror, holding the pencil with your dagger hand. The way the string hangs in relation to your arm will tell you whether your arm is perfectly straight or not.

High V. In the high V position, both arms are extended over your head in diagonal position. The effect, of course, is that your arms form both sides of the letter V. Variations of the high V include the low V, in which both arms are pointing down, and the broken high V and

LOOSEN UP BEFORE YOU PRACTICE

As with any physical activity, make sure your body is ready before you begin. Here are a few ways to warm up before practicing.

- Practice kicking as high as you can, first with one leg, then the other. Keep your legs and back straight as you kick. Do sets of 10 with each leg.

- Sit on the floor in a butterfly position, with your legs bent, the bottoms of your feet touching each other, and your back straight. Pull your feet in as close to your body as you can. Press down on your knees with your elbows for a count of 10.

- Standing up with your back straight, bend one leg behind you and grab your ankle. Hold the position for 30 seconds. Repeat with the other leg.

- Stand with your feet apart, wider than your shoulders. Bend slowly at the waist and reach for one of your ankles with both hands. Move your body to the middle so that one hand is on each ankle. Move your body to the other side so that both hands are reaching for the other ankle. Hold each position for about 30 seconds.

Work with your coach to develop a warm-up routine that loosens your muscles before every practice.

In the high V position, both arms are extended overhead to form the letter V.

broken low V, in which the arms are bent at the elbows. In all variations of the V, it's important to keep your arms stiff, your wrists tight, and your fists in a bucket position.

Let's Go Team Technique Tip: In the broken versions of the V, be sure to keep the pinkie sides of your fists facing forward.

Touchdown. Think of the touchdown as a double-arm punch up. You've probably seen referees at a football game signal a touchdown. That's exactly the kind of position you want to make. Make sure your elbows are locked and your fists are daggers. A variation of the touchdown is the low touchdown, in which your arms are pointing straight down to the ground. Your pinkie finger should face ahead.

Let's Go Team Technique Tip: Practice this motion in front of a mirror. Your arms will tend to veer off into a V position. Don't let them.

L. In the L position, your arms form the letter L. One arm will be pointing straight up, while the other arm will be pointing straight to the side. Whether the position is called a left L or a right L depends on which arm is pointing straight up in the air.

Let's Go Team Technique Tip: Practice holding your arms straight out with small weights, no more than five pounds maximum, in your hands. Then, when you do the L without holding a weight, it will seem a lot easier.

T. Like the L position, the T mimics the capital letter for which it is named. Your arms will be extended straight out to the sides. Usually the fists are in the bucket position, but they can be in the candlestick position, too. Like the broken diagonal, the broken T is a position in which the elbows are bent to create a shorter line with the arms.

Let's Go Team Technique Tip: Practicing in front of a mirror is crucial with the T, so that you're able to keep your arms in a very straight line parallel to the ground.

LEG MOTIONS

Now that you've learned some of the various fist and arm motions, here are some basic leg motions to get you started.

Feet together. This is the basic starting position for most cheerleaders. You simply need to be standing up

A cheerleading squad demonstrates the L position at the COA Nationals.

straight, but remember, posture is very important, so keep your back straight and your shoulders square. Make sure that the insides of your feet are touching each other. Feet apart is a slight variation in which you take a step to the left or right so that your feet are about shoulder width apart.

Let's Go Team Technique Tip: To work on keeping your back straight and your shoulders square, try practicing the feet together stance with your back against a wall.

Liberty hitch. In a liberty hitch, sometimes called a stag, lift one leg so that the inside of that leg's foot is even with your other leg's knee. Make sure that the toe of the

When one leg is lifted so that the foot is even with the other leg's knee, it is known as the liberty hitch leg position.

leg you're lifting is pointing down to the ground. Whether the move is known as a left liberty hitch or a right liberty hitch depends on which leg you're lifting. The side liberty hitch is a slight variation in which you simply turn your body to one side.

Let's Go Team Technique Tip: So that you have consistency in your liberty hitches, choose a spot on the instep or toe of your sneaker to match up with a spot on your knee, and concentrate on bringing the two spots together as you practice in front of a mirror.

Lunge. To do a lunge, start by standing with your back straight, facing forward. Set your feet wide apart, then move to one side, bending one leg so that the other leg is as straight as possible. The knee of your bent leg should be directly over your ankle. Whether you are doing a left lunge or a right lunge is determined by which leg you're bending.

Let's Go Team Technique Tip: Remember that the back foot—the one on the leg that's being extended—should face front, and it should create a 90-degree angle with the front foot—the one on the leg that's being bent.

Vocal Techniques

heerleading is more than simply a matter of physical movement. The first syllable in the word "cheerleading" is "cheer." So not only do you have to worry about getting your hands, arms, and legs into the proper positions, you also have to remember the cheers.

Where your voice is concerned, cheerleading has a lot in common with singing or acting. The most important thing to remember is that you want to project your voice. That means you want to be loud, so that you can be heard by everyone, but you don't want to screech.

Remember to cheer from your chest, not your throat. At first it might feel like your voice is deeper than it

Cheerleaders learn to project their voice from the chest and diaphragm, so they can be heard without screaming.

Proper voice control and enunciation are important if you want everyone to hear you cheer.

should be, but that's okay. Yelling from your lungs and your throat will make you loud, and it will make you heard, but it will also strain your voice and give you a sore throat. It's a waste of energy, and it's not the best way to be heard in the back row.

Work on projecting your voice from your chest and your diaphragm, the part of your body that separates the chest from the abdominal cavity. Your voice will be naturally louder, and the sound will carry farther. A big part of being able to do this is to breathe correctly from your diaphragm.

Proper enunciation of your cheers is important. You're trying to remember to smile for the crowd, so by doing so, you may throw off your speech patterns and the way you say things. Obviously, you want the words to be clear and understood by everyone in the crowd. If you can, try cheering into a tape recorder, then listen to your own voice. If you can't understand every word clearly, then you need to practice your enunciation. Sometimes it may feel like your mouth is being twisted into weird positions to get the words out the way you want them to sound.

BREATHE FROM THE DIAPHRAGM

You've probably heard it a thousand times: "Breathe from your diaphragm!" It's an important thing to remember whether you're a cheerleader, a singer, an actor, or anyone who wants to project their voice properly for a crowd.

How do you know if you're breathing properly? Here's an exercise to help you find out.

Place your hand on your belly button. When you breathe in, you should be feeling this area expand first, then spread upwards until your chest is expanded. Don't lift your shoulders. If you feel you are not breathing properly, lie flat on your back and place your hands on your waist, with your fingers pointing toward your belly button. Focus on filling up your stomach from the bottom to the top as you take a slow, deep breath. You should feel your stomach rise and your hands being raised gently up and outward until you feel your chest expanding.

That's okay. Practice in front of a mirror. You'll find that while it may feel unusual at first, it probably looks just fine.

Something you want to be aware of as a squad is for everyone to pronounce all the words in a cheer correctly. Let's say one of your school colors is orange, and you use the word "orange" in a cheer. One person may pronounce the word "ore-renge" while another person might pronounce it "are-ringe." It may sound like a slight

KEEP YOUR VOICE IN SHAPE!

To help keep your voice the absolute best it can be, follow these tips.

- Avoid places where there's a lot of secondhand cigarette or cigar smoke. The smoke will dry out your throat. Of course, you should never smoke yourself.

- Avoid drinking citrus juices like orange or grapefruit. They can affect your throat's lubrication. Less lubrication means you'll get a sore throat more easily.

- Don't eat a heavy meal before cheerleading. The food will sit in your stomach, and that will make it harder for you to properly control your breathing and the volume of your cheer.

- Avoid dairy products on a competition day. They tend to heavily coat the throat, which makes proper vocalizing more difficult.

- Drink plenty of water. If you're competing, drink water throughout the day up to the time of the competition. If you're cheering at a game, keep water on the sidelines and drink frequently.

difference, but think about it. There's a big difference between two people—or two halves of a cheerleading squad—saying any word two different ways at the same time, or saying it the same way all together. Obviously, if everyone says the word the same way, the squad will sound more unified, and the words in the cheer will be clearer to everyone in the stands.

Throughout this book, you're reminded of the importance of good posture. Correct posture is important for jumps and stunts, but it is important for your voice, too.

Be sure to keep your head up. If your head is down, it pinches off the throat and the sound can't get out as efficiently. Think of how a water hose pinched in the middle affects the flow of water out of the hose. Putting your head down has the same effect on the flow of sound. Also, if your head is down, your mouth is pointing down. That means your voice is being directed to the ground, not to the crowd that should be hearing what you're cheering.

Yes, cheering is a very physical activity. Don't forget about your voice, though. A healthy and powerful voice is a very important part of a successful cheerleader.

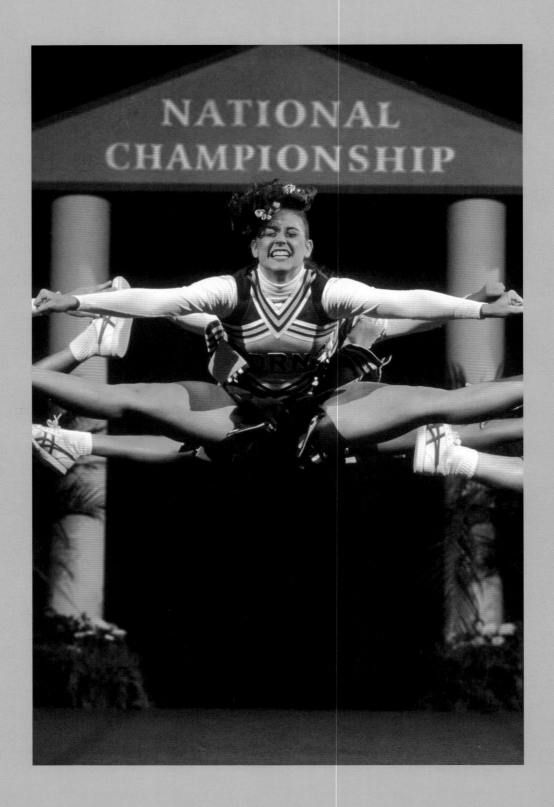

Jumps

Jumps are an important part of any cheerleading routine. They help maintain excitement and energy. They work very well during player introductions and are particularly appropriate after very exciting plays on the field. Well-executed jumps are eye-catching, and when a squad is able to jump in unison, it looks terrific to the crowd.

Any jump can be looked at as having three parts: the approach, the jump itself, and the landing.

THE APPROACH

Before you start working on actual jumps, work on your approach to the jump. The approach gets you into

Height isn't all that matters when it comes to jumps. Remember to keep your form, holding your upper body in position as well.

the air and gives your body the energy and momentum to get as high off the ground as possible.

Work on your approach by first standing on your toes with your arms in the high V. Keep your shoulders, head, and chest as high as you can. Next, bend your knees and bring your arms down quickly in front of you. Focus your body weight on the balls of your feet. Finally, jump straight up as hard as you can, swinging your arms so that they're both pointing straight up in the air. The combination of jumping with your legs and swinging your arms is what will give you the height you're looking for. Practice your approaches as much as you can. The better you're able to synchronize your arm and leg movements, the more height you'll achieve and the better your jump will be.

Practice your approaches in sets of five jumps, one right after the other. When you're jumping into the air, push off the ground as hard as you can. This will help you achieve maximum height in your jumps. Practice in front of a mirror so you can get the best coordination of arms and legs that will help you achieve the height you want.

Let's Go Team Technique Tip: Hold your head up high as you jump. This will make your jump appear to be several inches higher than it actually is.

THE LANDING

A good landing is important for two reasons. You want to land smoothly, in a position that's going to let you continue your routine without looking like you have to regain your footing before continuing. You also want to land in a way that minimizes the impact on your body.

You can limber up your jumping muscles and improve your jump height by doing lots of kicks.

As you practice your landings, remember that you never want your arms to be dangling at the end of a jump. Keep your knees slightly bent, flexible, and loose. Land so that your feet don't hit the ground flat-footed, which invites foot injuries. Land on the balls of your feet, rolling from toe to heel as you land. Keep your legs slightly bent and flexible, so that they absorb the impact of the landing.

Let's Go Team Technique Tip: Concentrate on your facial expression. The landing is when you're most likely to wince a little bit, so keep smiling.

TYPES OF JUMPS

There are several popular jumps that you might want to add to your cheerleading routines.

The Tuck. This is a great first jump to work on. It's simple, so you can concentrate on jump elements like getting good height, keeping your body straight, and landing properly and smoothly. Make fists with your hands. Jump

THE IMPORTANCE OF A PROPER LANDING

The human foot is incredibly complex. The foot contains 26 bones. That's one-fourth of all the bones in your entire body. The foot also contains 33 joints, 19 muscles, and 107 ligaments.

All these parts work together to give you the ability to walk, run, jump, and play. Because there's such complexity in the foot, one small problem in one area can cause further problems elsewhere in the foot. Problems in the feet can even affect the bones of the entire body.

That's why it's so important to practice proper landing techniques when you do your jumps. It's also crucial to have a good pair of sneakers. If your sneakers aren't comfortable, or if they're pinching your feet on the sides or the top, then it's time to think about getting new ones.

straight in the air. When you do so, keep your knees and feet together, bring your knees up toward your chest, and raise your arms in a high V. Work on keeping your back straight, your thighs parallel to the ground, and your toes pointed straight down.

Let's Go Team Technique Tip: Try curling your toes as you jump, that will help make your feet point straight down like they should.

The Spread Eagle. Jump straight in the air and spread your legs out to the sides while holding your arms in the high V position. Remember to point your toes, and to keep your legs straight. Make daggers with your hands. Like the tuck, this is a simple jump, but you'll want to practice it a lot so you can get the feel of how to position your arms and legs properly while doing any kind of jump. When practicing the spread eagle, try working in front of a mirror and positioning your arms and legs so that the effect is like a giant capital X.

Let's Go Team Technique Tip: Don't spread your legs or arms too far apart, or the effect of the "X" will be lost.

The Front Hurdler. The front hurdler is a jump in which one leg is extended straight out in front of you and the other leg is bent at the knee and pulled up behind you. The effect looks like a runner jumping over a hurdle, hence the name. Keep your back straight, hold your arms in a high V, and remember to point your feet so that the sole of your back foot is parallel to the floor, and the toe of your front foot is pointing straight down to the floor. As you land, bring your feet together and finish in a standing position.

No matter what kind of jump you attempt, remember that form is always more important than height.

Let's Go Team Technique Tip: When you practice, focus on a spot in front of you and try to kick as high as that spot. Keep moving the spot higher as you work on the jump.

The Double Hook. Sometimes referred to as a pinwheel or an abstract, the double hook jump is similar to a hurdler, except that both legs are bent at the knees, one in front of your body and one behind your body. Keep your back straight, make fists with your hands, and maintain your arms in a high V position.

Let's Go Team Technique Tip: Be sure to land straight and with your feet together, not hunched over.

The Herkie. This jump is named after Lawrence Herkimer, who started the first cheerleading company and ran the first cheerleading camp in the 1940s. It's also commonly called the side hurdler. When performing the

Herkie, you kick one leg out straight to the side so that it's parallel with the ground, and you bend your other leg so that the knee is pointing to the ground. Sometimes the Herkie is performed with the knee of the bent leg facing to the front rather than down to the ground. Make fists with your hands.

Let's Go Team Technique Tip: Be sure to keep your bent leg tucked in tight against your body.

The Toe Touch. This is one of the most popular jumps that cheerleaders do. It's also one of the most difficult to master. When you jump, you'll be stretching your arms straight out to your sides, and doing the same with your

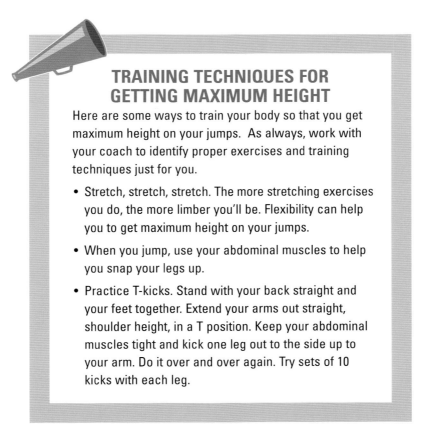

TRAINING TECHNIQUES FOR GETTING MAXIMUM HEIGHT

Here are some ways to train your body so that you get maximum height on your jumps. As always, work with your coach to identify proper exercises and training techniques just for you.

- Stretch, stretch, stretch. The more stretching exercises you do, the more limber you'll be. Flexibility can help you to get maximum height on your jumps.

- When you jump, use your abdominal muscles to help you snap your legs up.

- Practice T-kicks. Stand with your back straight and your feet together. Extend your arms out straight, shoulder height, in a T position. Keep your abdominal muscles tight and kick one leg out to the side up to your arm. Do it over and over again. Try sets of 10 kicks with each leg.

The toe touch is one of the most difficult jumps to learn. Make sure you bring your legs up to your arms, and not vice versa.

legs. Keep your hands open, palms flat and facing the ground. Keep your arms parallel with the ground, and bring your legs up so that you're almost touching your toes. Bringing your legs up is an important point to remember. You can achieve the same position by bringing your body down, but the overall jump won't be as high.

Let's Go Team Technique Tip: Remember to keep your head, chest, and shoulders high, point your toes, and keep your knees and sneaker laces facing up.

The Double-9. The double-9 is an interesting jump, because your body creates exactly what the name of the jump is called. To do a double-9, you'll want to bend at the waist and extend your left arm and left leg straight forward. Make fists with your hands. Bend your right arm at the elbow and bring your right hand to your left biceps. Bend your right leg at the knee and bring your right foot to your left thigh, just above the knee. Your arm position should mirror your leg position. The effect for the person watching the jump is that your arms are forming a "9" and your legs are forming a "9" too.

Let's Go Team Technique Tip: To get the best height, be sure to bring your legs to your arms, not your arms to your legs.

As you work on your jumps, you'll probably find yourself concentrating on getting as high into the air as possible. That's fine. Remember, though, that jumping is about more than just height. It's about overall form, and proper approach and landing techniques. Don't sacrifice the whole jump just for the sake of trying to maximize your height.

Stunts

 good way to think of stunting is to break stunts into two broad categories. There are partner stunts, which involve two people, and mounts, often called pyramids, which involve three or more people.

In any stunt, there are three types of participants: bases, flyers, and spotters.

The base is the bottom person in the stunt, and the base's feet will be on the ground. The base supports the flyer, so it's important that the base be strong and able to stay still and balanced at all times.

The flyer, sometimes called the "mounter," is the person who is elevated into the air. The flyer tends to be

Bases face each other for the prep, in which they hold a flyer up with her feet in their hands. The back spotter assists in both the mount and dismount.

Stunts involving three or more people are known as mounts or pyramids.

smaller and lighter than the base and needs to have excellent body control. The flyer must be aware of where her body weight is at all times. The flyer should never be pushing or pulling the base off balance.

In addition to bases and flyers, stunts should always include spotters. It is a spotter's main responsibility to make sure that in the event of an accident, the flyer's head does not hit the ground. Beyond this responsibility, the spotter needs to know every aspect of the cheering routine. When the spotter knows the routine, she knows where the dangerous points in the routine are, and she can intensify her efforts to help insure the safety of everyone on the squad. In many stunts, multiple spotters are utilized, and a back spotter is designated as the primary catcher of the flyer, so back spotters need to be strong, confident, and able to handle fast-moving weight.

In this chapter, we'll look at several basic stunts in the categories of partner stunts and mounts, just to get you started and give you a sense of what's involved in stunting. For more, be sure to discuss stunting with your coach, and refer to such books as *The Official Cheerleaders Handbook* and *Ultimate Cheerleading.*

WARNING! Before trying any stunting, be sure to have an expert coach or trainer watching, and always use spotters. Stunting can be extremely dangerous. Even a stunt that looks very simple and safe can cause injury if done improperly. Don't take any chances. Cheer safely.

PARTNER STUNTS

The Pony Mount. Sometimes called the pony sit, the pony mount is probably the easiest partner stunt there is. Because of that, it's a good one to start with so you can think less about technique and body positioning and more about getting comfortable with the idea of stunting and working with another person.

(1) The base bends her knees slightly and stands with her feet shoulder width apart. Her hands should be braced against her thighs, just above the knees. Her elbows should be locked, and her back should be flat and rigid.

(2) The flyer stands directly behind the base and places one hand on the base's lower back, and the other hand on the base's shoulder.

(3) Using her arms to support her weight as she jumps, the flyer hops into a sitting position on the base's back. The flyer's knees are bent so that her feet are tucked in behind the base and pointing to the back.

(4) Once she is sitting on the base's back, the flyer raises her arms in a high V position.

(5) To dismount, the flyer hops down as the base stands up straight. Both cheerleaders return to the hands on hips position.

Let's Go Team Technique Tip: Both cheerleaders should have their heads up, facing forward, maintaining eye contact with the crowd.

The Side Stand. The side stand is a simple one-step stunt, but it's a good one to help you start focusing your attention on form. The flyer needs to focus on stepping onto the base and assuming the T position with a sense of effortlessness. In all stunting, the goal is to make it look easy, not complicated. Your movements should be smooth and coordinated. Your expression should never look strained.

(1) The base stands in a right lunge position, while the flyer stands behind the base's right leg and places her left foot on the base's right thigh.

(2) The flyer steps up onto the base's thigh with both feet and assumes the T position, remembering to keep her feet together. The base wraps her right arm behind the

flyer's knees and rests her hand just above the flyer's right knee to provide extra support.

(3) To dismount, the flyer steps back or forward while the base remains still and uses her right arm to help guide the flyer back to the ground.

Let's Go Team Technique Tip: The base needs to remember to keep the knee of her bent leg positioned over her foot. The flyer needs to concentrate on her body weight so

THE DANGERS OF STUNTING

Stunting can be dangerous if it is not done properly. Some stunts, such as the dive roll—a forward roll in which a cheerleader is airborne before the completion of the roll—have been declared illegal by organizations like the National Cheerleading Association and the National Federation of State High School Associations.

Many school and cheerleading organizations strictly prohibit the types of stunts that may be used by squads at certain levels. Often, the types of stunts a squad may do are limited, depending on whether the squad is competing at a freshman, sophomore, junior, or senior level.

According to the National Center for Catastrophic Sport Injury Research, cheerleading leads to more serious injuries to women than traditional sports such as gymnastics and track. That's no reason to panic, though. According to the American Association of Cheerleading Coaches and Advisers, "National injury estimates clearly show that compared to other athletic activities, cheerleading has one of the lowest occurrences of injury that leads to an emergency room visit."

The lesson is clear. When stunting, be sure to use spotters. Cheer safely and responsibly.

she remains balanced and still and appears poised and confident.

The Shoulder Stand. Now we're starting to really get into the air. Be absolutely sure to have a spotter on hand before you start working on this partner stunt.

(1) The base stands in a right lunge position in front of the flyer and, extending her arms above her head, reaches out and back with her arms to join hands with those of the flyer.

(2) The flyer steps onto the base's right thigh with her right foot, pushes off the ground, locks the knee of her right leg, and places her left foot on the base's left shoulder.

(3) As the base provides support with her arms, the flyer presses down on her left foot and brings her right foot up onto the base's right shoulder.

(4) The base releases the flyer's hands one hand at a time, and places her hands behind the flyer's calves to provide extra balance and support. As the base straightens her knees, the flyer stands up straight and assumes a high V or hands on hips position.

(5) To dismount, the flyer steps forward, off the base's shoulders. The base helps the flyer to the ground by catching the flyer at the waist with both hands. The flyer should remember to keep her knees bent and flexible as she hits the ground to minimize the impact of the dismount.

Let's Go Team Technique Tip: Remember to keep your eyes looking forward, not down. The base should pull forward slightly with the hands and lean back slightly

Never try stunting until you have been taught the moves properly by your coach or trainer. For your safety, it is also essential to use spotters at all times.

with the head to provide a bit of extra support to the flyer. The flyer should remember to distribute her weight evenly on both feet.

MOUNTS

The Double Lunge. Think of this mount as a variation of the side stand partner stunt, except that it utilizes two bases and not one. The double lunge is a good mount for three cheerleaders to practice when focusing on teamwork and the ability to work together to present a mount without looking strained. Once perfected, it can also be used as a starting point for more sophisticated mounts.

(1) The two bases lunge toward each other, making sure their hips are turned to the front. The feet of their bent legs should be positioned so that one is in front of the other.

(2) The flyer places her hands on the bases' shoulders, and places her foot onto the upper thigh of one of the

IMPORTANT TIPS FOR ALL STUNTS

Whether you're working on partner stunts or mounts, here are some important tips to remember.

- Keep your head up and look confident. You don't want to appear as if you're struggling to assume the stunt position.

- Have everyone on your squad agree on a signal word, such as "STOP." This way, if a flyer needs to dismount unexpectedly, the bases and spotters will be ready.

- Wear snug clothing. Arms and legs can get snagged on loose or baggy shirts and pants, which can mean injuries.

- Tie up your hair, cut your nails, and don't wear any jewelry.

- Never talk during a stunt. Everyone participating in the stunt needs to remain focused on the job at hand.

- Always remember to keep your weight distributed evenly, whether you are a base or a flyer.

- If you feel uncomfortable about doing a particular stunt, don't do it.

- Don't forget the importance of warming up before stunting. Participating in stunting without warming up can be dangerous.

bases. The base who is being stepped on first should wrap her arm around the ankle of the flyer.

(3) The flyer steps up with her bent leg, and places her other foot on the upper thigh of the other base, who wraps her arm around the flyer's ankle. Standing up straight, the flyer locks her knees and raises her arms in a high V while the bases maintain their free arms in a hands on hips position.

(4) To dismount, the flyer holds hands with the bases' free hands and jumps to the front.

Let's Go Team Technique Tip: When doing the double lunge the bases should both bend their legs at the same angle so that the stunt doesn't look lopsided. When wrapping their arms around the flyer's ankle, the bases can use the insides of their elbows to provide additional support to the flyer's legs.

The Prep. This stunt requires two bases, one flyer, and a back spotter. Like the double lunge, it can serve as a stepping stone to more sophisticated stunts once it's learned and perfected.

(1) The two bases should stand facing each other in front of the flyer with their feet shoulder's width apart. The back spotter should be positioned directly behind the flyer.

(2) The two bases in front squat down, keeping their backs straight and their feet firm on the floor. They hold their hands together, keeping their elbows tucked in toward their bodies.

(3) The flyer places her hands on the bases' shoulders and hops up, keeping her feet together as she jumps into

When doing stunts, the goal is to make it look effortless.
Don't forget to smile and make it look like the move is easy.

the bases' hands. The bases should get a firm grip on the toes and heels of the flyer's feet.

(4) Standing together, the bases bring their hands up to chin level. The flyer locks her legs and stands up straight.

(5) To dismount, the bases bend their knees slightly, then, on the back spotter's signal, pop their arms into the

air, tossing the flyer slightly into the air so that she can kick her legs to the front. The bases extend their arms to catch the flyer in a cradle catch. In a cradle catch, the bases catch the flyer both under the thighs and behind the back, forming a sort of cradle with both sets of arms.

Let's Go Team Technique Tip: The back spotter is essential in this stunt and should hold the flyer's waist and assist in both the mount and the dismount. At no time should the side bases use their backs to lift the flyer. They should always lift with legs and arms. The flyer should keep her feet shoulder width at all times and should maintain a tight body throughout the stunt, never being loose or wobbly.

Don't Forget
the Attitude

ou have the hand, arm, and leg positions mastered. Your diaphragm breathing is perfect. You've perfected every jump and stunt there is to know, but you still have more to remember.

Whether you're trying out for a squad or appearing in front of judges during a competition, your attitude is going to count. Here are some tips to remember when you're on the cheerleading floor.

Smile. You don't want to look like you have a fake smile plastered on your face, but you do want to remember to smile naturally. It's a simple thing, but sometimes it's hard to remember. You're a cheerleader, though, and that

It takes a lot of practice to be able to cheer, smile, and maintain eye contact with the judges or audience at the same time.

Crisp movements are the sign of a good cheerleader, so don't get sloppy just because the move is easy.

means you want to present a positive and enthusiastic face to the world. Smile, make cheerful facial expressions, wink, show your enthusiasm (without overdoing it). Don't be afraid to let those emotions shine through.

Maintain eye contact. Eye contact is a great way to communicate with your audience. It tells them you're performing for them. It's also a great way to remind yourself to keep your head up.

Be crisp in your movements. When you're striking your poses and doing your chants and cheers, be as crisp as possible in your movements. You don't want the audience to think you didn't get any sleep the night before. You also don't want to look like you don't have enough energy to get through the routine. As a cheerleader, you're there to set a standard for enthusiasm.

DO YOU HAVE THE RIGHT ATTITUDE?

Nobody expects anybody to be perfect, and that goes for cheerleaders, too. However, people do expect cheerleaders to be role models of good behavior and a positive attitude. Do you have the right attitude to be a cheerleader? For each statement below, answer yes or no.

- I hardly ever argue with my friends in anger.
- I maintain a high standard for myself where grades are concerned.
- People generally say I'm a positive person.
- My classmates look at me as someone who is willing to be helpful.
- My teachers generally have nice things to say about me.
- I'm not embarrassed to stand up in front of the classroom and speak.
- I think that having school spirit and loyalty is a good thing.
- I like to keep my appearance neat and clean.

If you answered "yes" to six or more statements, you are well on your way to having the positive attitude of a great cheerleader!

Show dedication. Demonstrate for your coach, the judges, and most of all for yourself, that you're there to do your best. If you're truly dedicated, if you show up on time for practices, if you practice at home, if you work really hard at being a cheerleader, and you're not just on the team for the sake of wearing the uniform, that dedication will naturally show through.

Remember the uniform. Remember, when you're wearing a cheerleading uniform, you're representing your school or your squad. Consider it an honor. Remember, too, that anything negative you do will reflect on your fellow squad members, and perhaps even your school. Most of all, it reflects on you, so show yourself—as well as your friends and classmates—the proper respect.

KEEP IT NEAT

Many squads and competitions have specific rules about a cheerleader's appearance. Here are some of the most common rules.

- No jewelry while cheering. This includes earrings, necklaces, bracelets, and belly button rings.

- No loose-hanging hair. Any long hair should be pulled back off the face and kept back in a tight ponytail.

- No heavy makeup. Lip or nail colors must be clear or pastel only.

- No gum chewing while cheering.

- Uniforms should be clean and neatly pressed and should include plain white socks and clean white cheerleading sneakers.

Don't forget to smile. You should be having fun, and you want that to show through your cheering.

Respect the other team. When cheering at a game, remember that you're cheering for your team, not against the other team. When cheering at a competition, remember that you're there to do your best, and you should not take any pleasure in another squad's misfortunes.

Have fun. Sure, there's a lot to remember. Getting the arm and leg movements just right, maximizing the height of your jumps, looking just right, and on and on and on. When all is said and done, though, if you're not having fun, what's the point of all the hard work?

Glossary

abstract – Another term for a double hook jump.

arch – A position in which the back is curved.

back spotter – A spotter whose role is to serve as the primary catcher of a flyer.

base – The bottom person in a stunt who remains in contact with the floor. The base supports the mounter in a stunt.

basket toss – A toss of a flyer into the air that involves three or more tossers, two of whom have their hands interlocked.

blade – A hand position in which the hand is opened flat and all the fingers are pressed together.

bucket – A hand position in which the fingers form a fist that faces the ground as if the person were carrying a bucket of water.

candlestick – A hand position in which the fingers form a fist that's turned to the side as if the hand were holding a candlestick.

chant – A short, repetitive yell performed continually throughout a game (example: "De-fense! De-fense!"), or a short routine with words sometimes involving the crowd.

cheer – A longer, more spirited yell that is performed only during official breaks of a game. Often, a cheer will utilize a variety of motions and stunts.

cradle catch – A method of catching a flyer by holding her around the back and under the thighs.

dagger – A hand position in which the fingers form a fist and the fist is held such that it looks like you are stabbing the air with an imaginary dagger.

diagonal – An arm position in which both arms are extended, but one arm is raised and the other lowered, with the effect being that both arms create a straight line diagonal to the body.

dismount – The act of safely returning to a floor position following a stunt.

double hook – A type of jump in which both legs are bent at the knees. The double hook jump is sometimes referred to as a pinwheel or abstract.

flyer – The person who is elevated into the air by bases to perform a mount. The flyer is sometimes called a mounter.

hands on hips – An arm position in which both hands are clasped into fists, and the fists are placed exactly opposite each other on the hips.

handspring – A spring from a standing position to the hands, and back to a standing position.

Herkie – Named for Lawrence Herkimer, this is a type of jump in which one leg is straight and the other leg is bent. The Herkie is also called the side hurdler.

high V – An arm position in which both arms are extended overhead to form the letter V.

hurdler – A type of jump in which one leg is extended straight forward and the other leg is bent to the side.

jump – A spring into the air in which both feet leave the ground and the body assumes a given position.

L – An arm position in which one arm points straight up, while the other arm points out to the side, forming the letter L.

liberty hitch – A leg movement in which one leg is lifted so that the inside of that leg's foot is even with the other leg's knee; the liberty hitch is also called a stag.

lunge – A leg movement in which the feet are set wide apart, then the person moves in one direction, bending one leg so that the other leg is as straight as possible. The knee of the bent leg should be directly over that leg's ankle.

mid-base – A base who is not in contact with the ground or other performance surface.

mount – Often used interchangeably with "stunt," a mount is any skill in which one or more people are supported in the air.

mounter – Another term for a flyer.

pinwheel – Another term for a double hook jump.

pony mount – A partner stunt in which the flyer sits on the base's back.

punch up – An arm motion in which one arm "punches" the air so that your arm finishes extended straight up with the hand held in a fist.

pyramid – A stunt involving one or more flyers supported by one or more bases and linked together.

routine – A choreographed sequence of moves.

shoulder stand – A partner stunt in which the flyer stands atop the base's shoulders.

side hurdler – Another name for the Herkie jump.

side stand – A simple one-step partner stunt in which the flyer stands atop the base, who is performing a lunge.

split – A position in which the legs are spread apart in alignment or sideways, one in front of the other.

spotter – A person who is in direct contact with the floor and may help control the building of, or dismounting from, a mount. This person may not provide primary support for the mount, meaning that the mount or pyramid would remain stable without the spotter. The primary responsibility of the spotter is to watch for safety hazards. The spotter is positioned on the floor in such a way as to prevent injuries, with particular concern to the head, neck, and back areas.

spread eagle – A type of jump in which the arms and legs are spread out to form a giant letter X.

stag – A leap or pose in which one leg is bent and the other is straight; also called a liberty hitch.

straddle – A position where the legs are straight out and apart.

stunt – Any maneuver that includes tumbling, mounting, a pyramid, or a toss.

T – An arm position in which both arms are extended straight out to the sides, forming the letter T.

toss – A throwing motion by the base or bases to increase the height of the top person in the mount, during which the top person has no contact at all with the base or bases.

touchdown – An arm motion in which both arms are pointing straight up, in the manner of a referee signaling a touchdown.

transition – A choreographed maneuver that enables a team to move from one highlighted stunt to the next.

tuck – A type of jump during which the knees are brought up and held tightly to the chest.

tumbling – Gymnastic skills used in cheerleading.

Internet Resources

http://cheerleading.about.com/index.htm
An About.com directory of hundreds of Web sites, categorized by headings like Cheerleading 101, Cheers and Chants, and Fundraising.

http://www.aacca.org/aacca/guidelines.htm
Cheerleading safety guidelines from the American Association of Cheerleading Coaches and Advisers. Two sets of guidelines are provided: one for high school level, and one for college level.

http://www.americancheerleader.com
The official Web site of *American Cheerleader* magazine features message boards, chat, and a wide variety of articles available to subscribers.

http://www.cheerhome.com
CheerHome.com features news, message boards, articles, and resources for learning more about cheerleading activities.

http://www.cheerleading.net
Cheerleading.net has links to hundreds of Web sites for cheerleaders and coaches at all levels.

http://www.cheerleading.org.uk
The Web site of the British Cheerleading Association has information about championships, camps, and clinics in the United Kingdom.

http://www.nationalspirit.com/home.asp
The National Spirit Group is the parent company of the National Cheerleaders Association, founded in 1948 by Lawrence Herkimer.

http://www.varsity.com
Varsity.com offers information on cheerleading and dance. The Universal Cheerleaders Association (UCA), a leader in cheerleading safety and stunt innovation, is also part of Varsity.com. The UCA is one of the largest cheerleading camp providers and competition sponsors in the world.

Further Reading

Chappell, Linda Rae. *Coaching Cheerleading Successfully.* Champaign, Illinois: Human Kinetics, 1997.

French, Stephanie Breaux. *The Cheerleading Book.* Chicago: Contemporary Books, 1995.

Kuch, K.D. *The Cheerleaders Almanac.* New York: Random House, 1996.

McElroy, James T. *We've Got Spirit: The Life and Times of America's Greatest Cheerleading Team.* New York: Berkley Books, 1999.

Neil, Randy, and Elaine Hart. *The Official Cheerleader's Handbook.* New York: Fireside Books, 1986.

Rusconi, Ellen. *Cheerleading.* Danbury, Connecticut: Children's Press, 2001.

Scott, Kieran. *Ultimate Cheerleading.* New York: Scholastic, Inc., 1998.

Index

CRAIG PETERS has been writing about various aspects of sports and popular culture for more than two decades. His daughter, Alexandra, began her dance and cheerleading training when she was two years old. By the age of 13, Alexandra had competed on several school and recreation teams and been named captain of her middle school cheerleading squad. Craig has long ago given up the idea that this might be a passing fad for his daughter.